THIS BOOK BELONGS TO

Once upon a time,

in the small village of Maplewood,

there was a little squirrel

named Sammy.

Sammy was known

for his fluffy tail,

quick feet,

and love for nuts.

Every day, he would scurry

around the village,

gathering acorns

and playing with his friends.

But there was one thing

Sammy often forgot to do—say

"thank you."

One sunny morning, Sammy's friend Daisy the Duck offered him a shiny, red apple she had found near the farmer's market.

Sammy grabbed the apple, munched on it quickly, and ran off to play without saying a word. Daisy felt a little sad but didn't say anything.

Later that day, Benny the Bunny helped Sammy find his missing acorn stash. Benny had spent a long time hopping around and searching.

When he finally found the acorns under a big oak tree, he called out to Sammy with excitement.

Sammy quickly took the acorns and dashed off, forgetting to say "thank you" to Benny.

That evening, the animals gathered for their nightly storytelling session.

Mrs. Owl, the wise old storyteller, noticed that Sammy was all alone.

Curious, she asked, "Sammy, why are you not playing with your friends?"

Sammy shrugged and replied, "I don't know. They just seem upset with me today."

Mrs. Owl looked at Sammy kindly and said, "Sometimes, it's not what you do, but what you don't do that matters.

Have you remembered to say 'thank you' today?"

Sammy thought for a moment and realized he hadn't said "thank you" at all.

Not to Daisy for the apple, nor to Benny for finding his acorns.

Feeling embarrassed, he asked Mrs. Owl, "Does saying 'thank you' really make such a difference?"

Mrs. Owl nodded wisely and told Sammy a story about a magic word that could make others feel warm and happy inside.

She explained that saying "thank you" shows that you appreciate what others do for you, no matter how small.

"Gratitude," she said, "is just like a little seed that grows into a big tree of kindness."

Determined to make things right, Sammy decided to find his friends the next day.

The first stop was Daisy's pond.

Sammy spotted her swimming around.

He approached her and said, "Daisy, I'm really sorry I forgot to thank you for the apple.

It was delicious. Thank you for being so kind."

Daisy's eyes brightened up, and she quacked happily, "

Oh, Sammy, that means a lot to me!

Thank you for saying that."

Next, Sammy hopped over to Benny's burrow.

He found Benny munching on a carrot.

"Benny," Sammy began, "I'm sorry I didn't thank you for helping me find my acorns.

It was very helpful, and I'm grateful."

Benny smiled widely
and replied, "Thanks, Sammy.

I'm glad you said that.

Let's play together again!"

From that day on, Sammy made a point to always say "thank you" whenever someone helped him or gave him something.

He noticed that the more he said it, the happier his friends seemed, and the more they wanted to play with him and help each other out.

The village of Maplewood became even friendlier, with all the animals practicing the magic of gratitude.

And so, Sammy learned that two simple words—"thank you"—could make a big difference.

They brought friends closer, spread kindness, and made everyone feel good inside.

He continued to share his newfound knowledge with everyone, reminding them that gratitude can make the world a little brighter.

THE END

www.ingramcontent.com/pod-product-compliance
Lightning Source LLC
Chambersburg PA
CBHW041822110726
48006CB00019B/2471

9798330387366